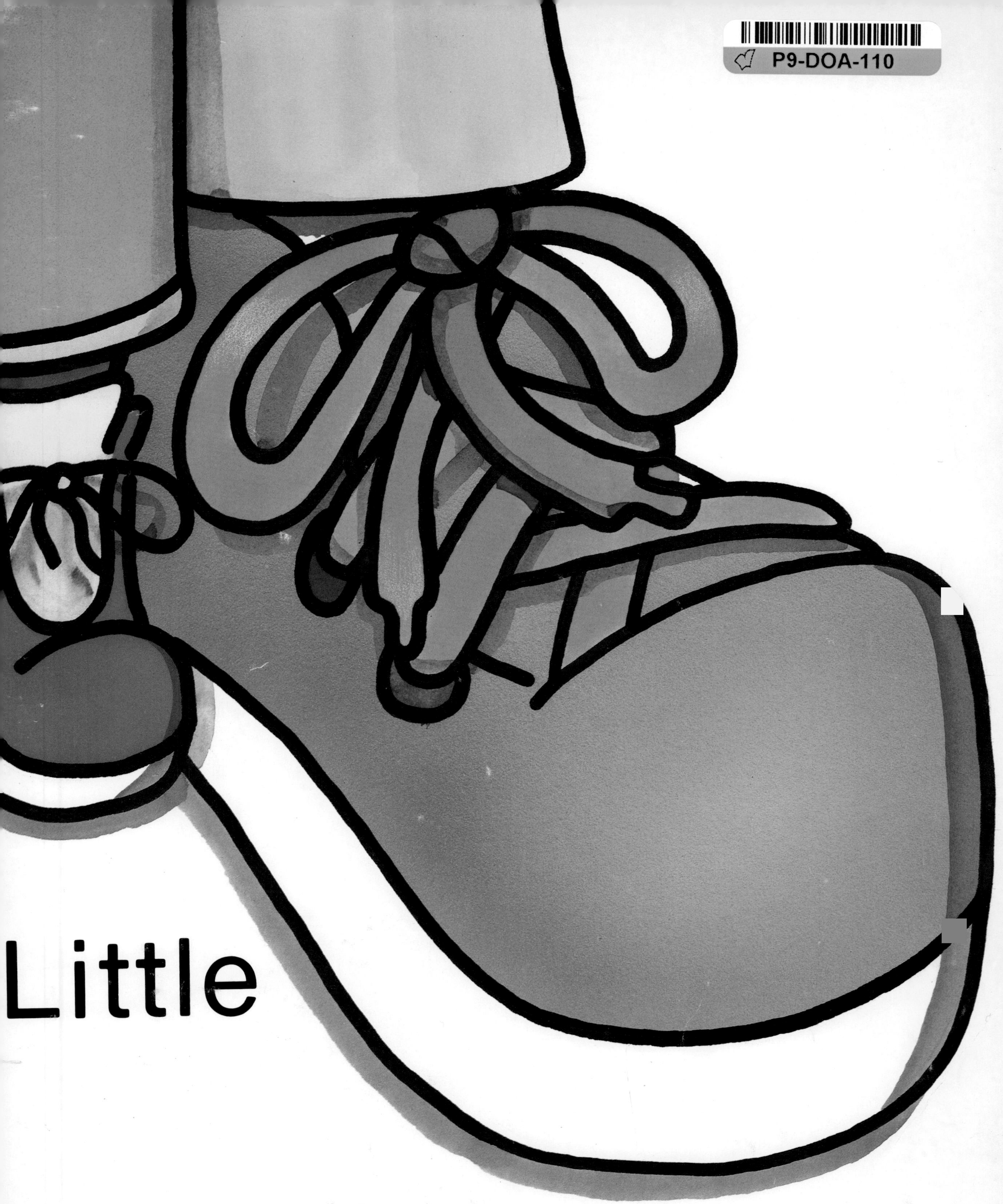

Little

Huge

Tiny

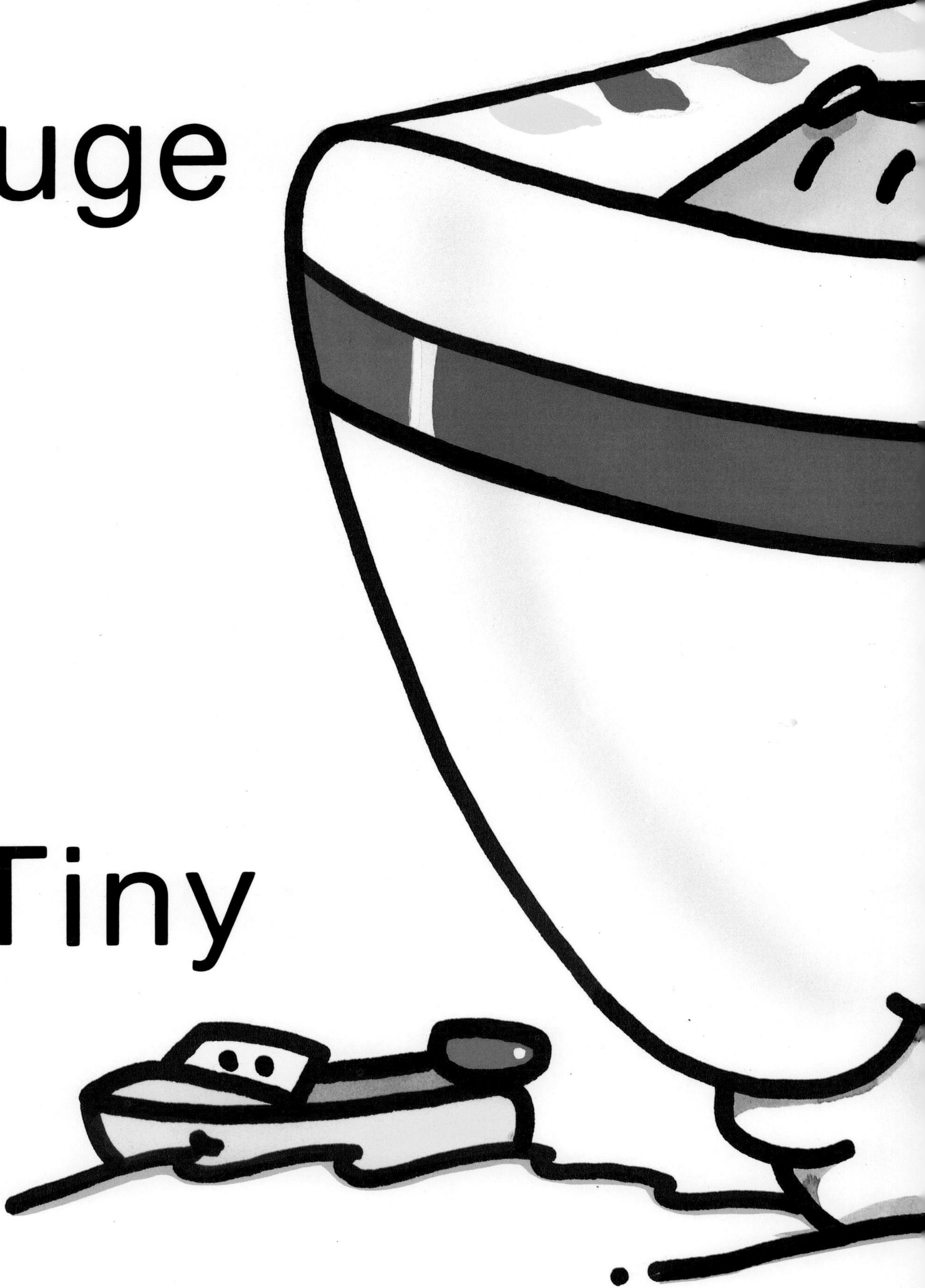

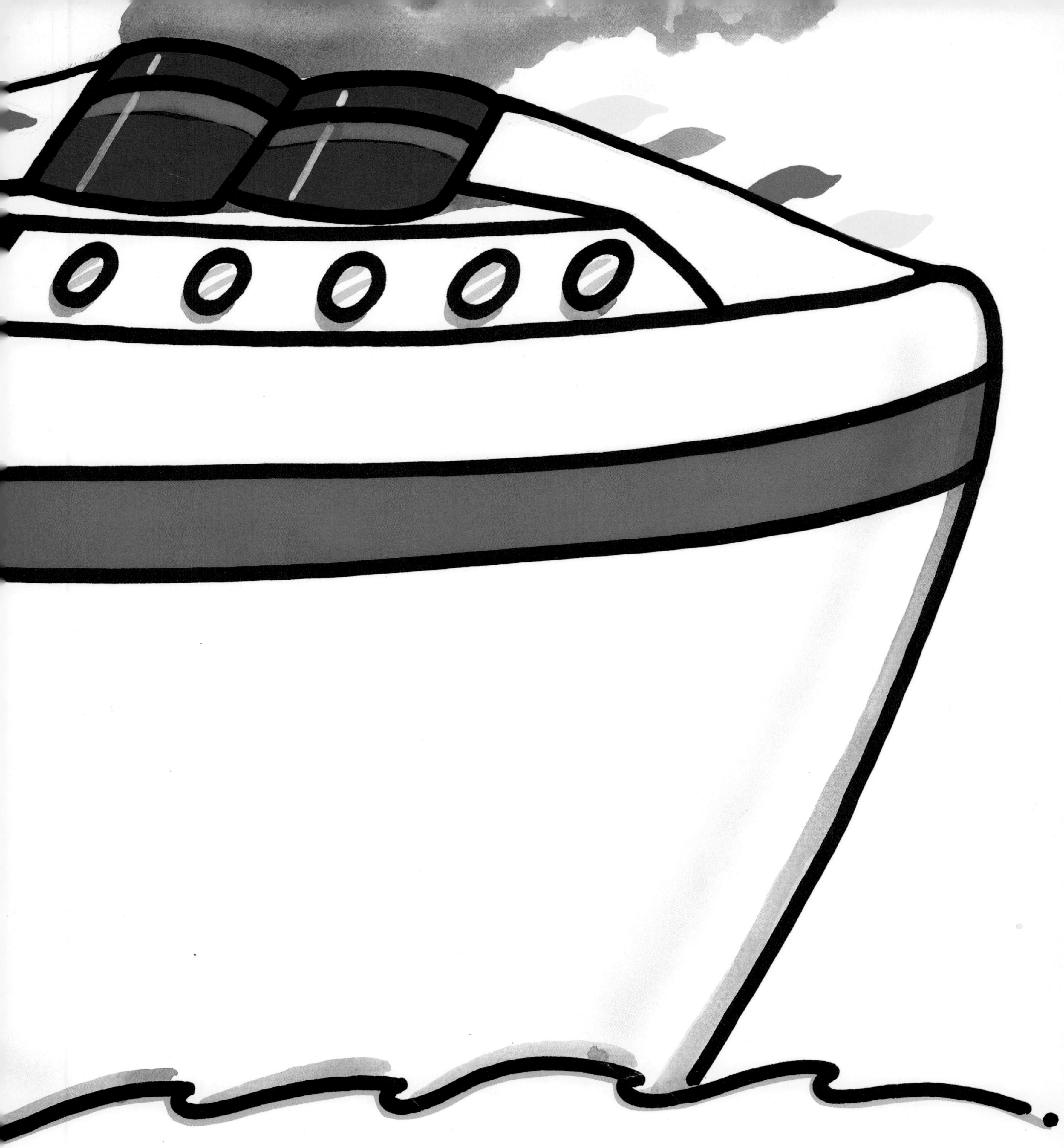

Short

Long

Big

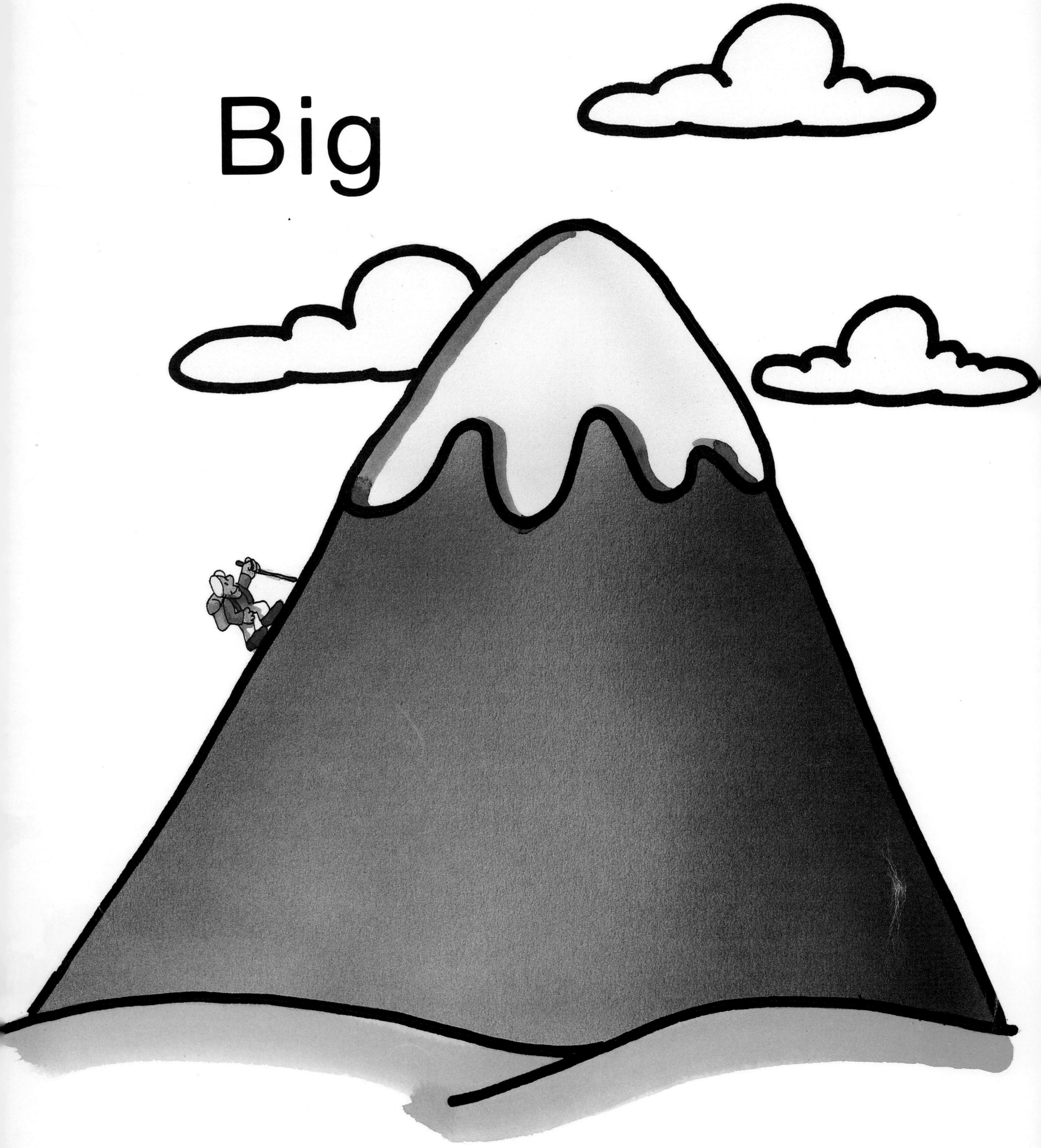

Little

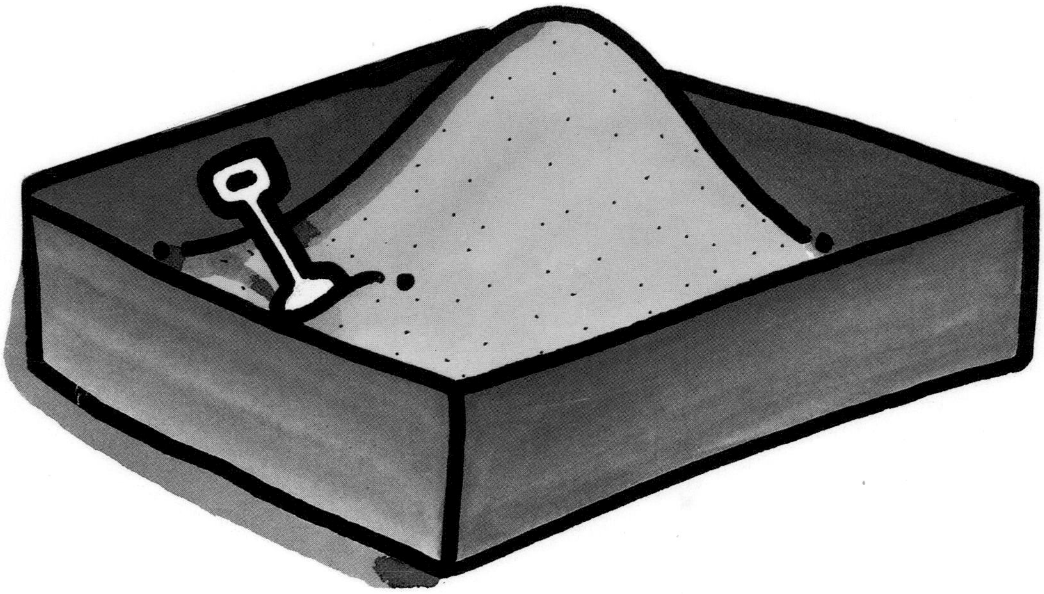

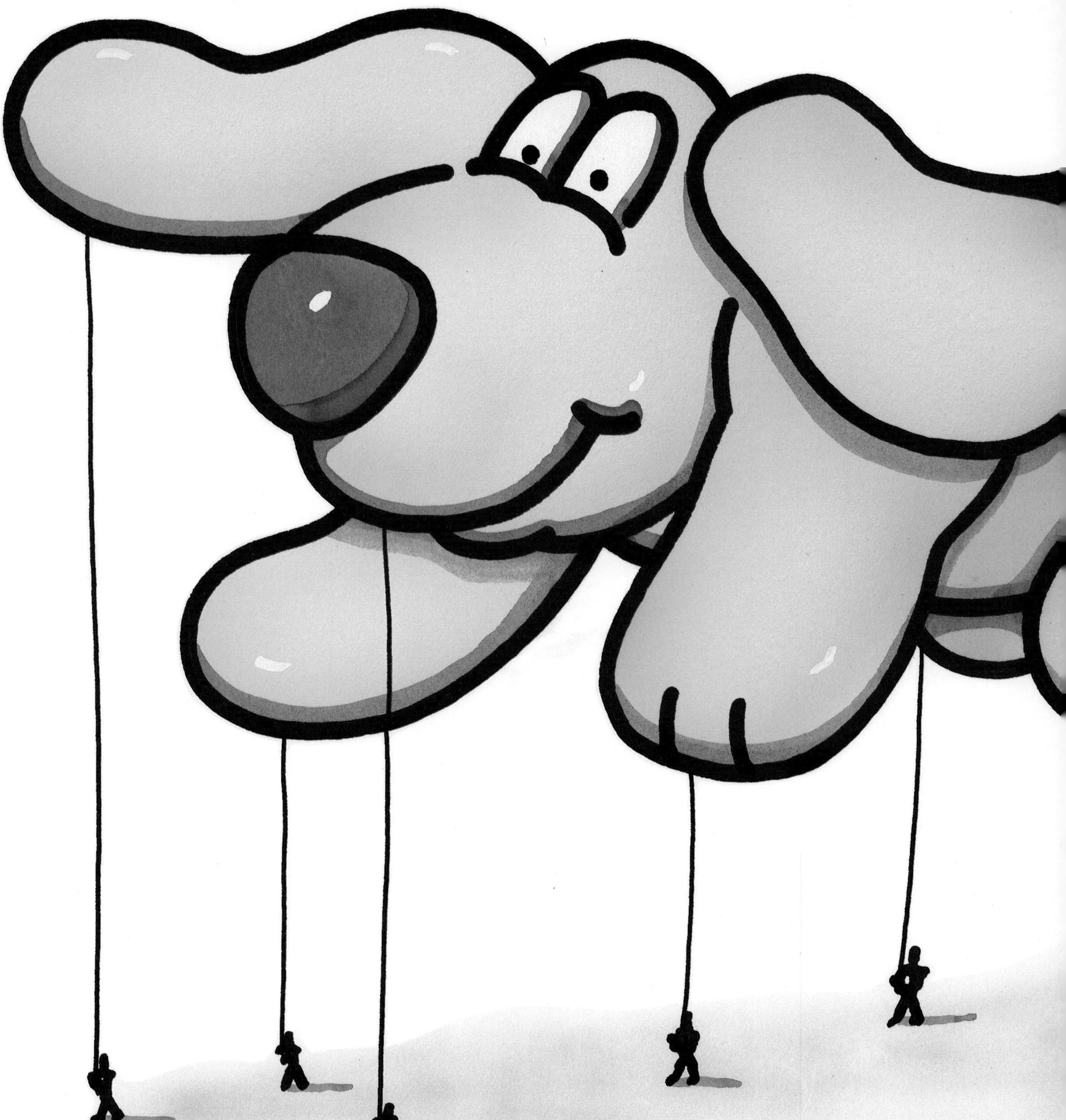

Huge

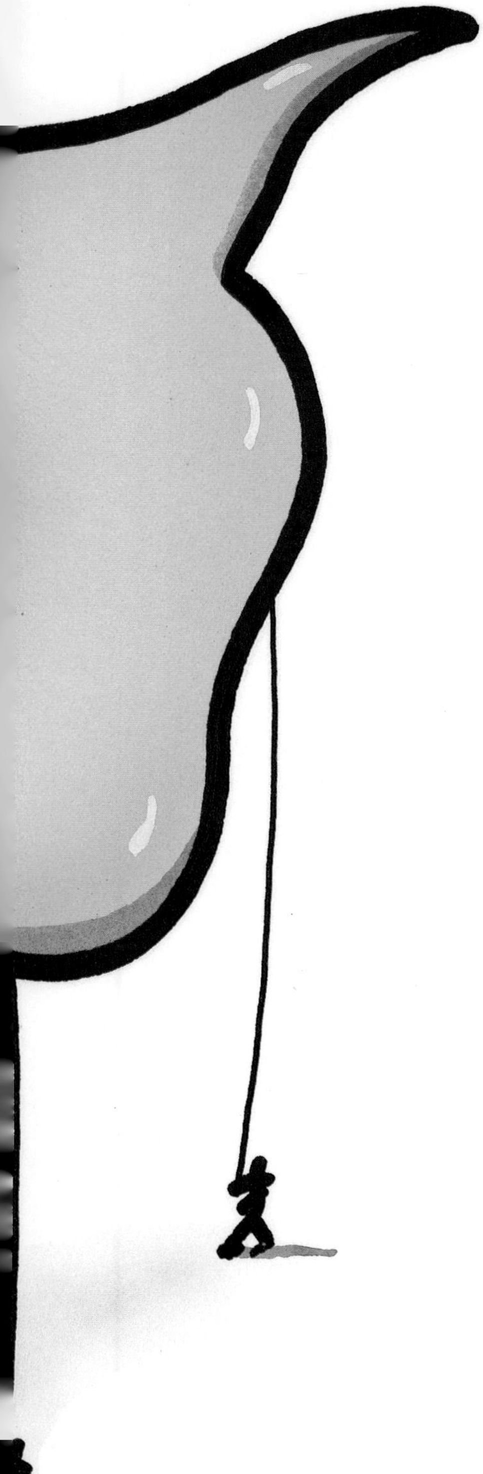

Tiny

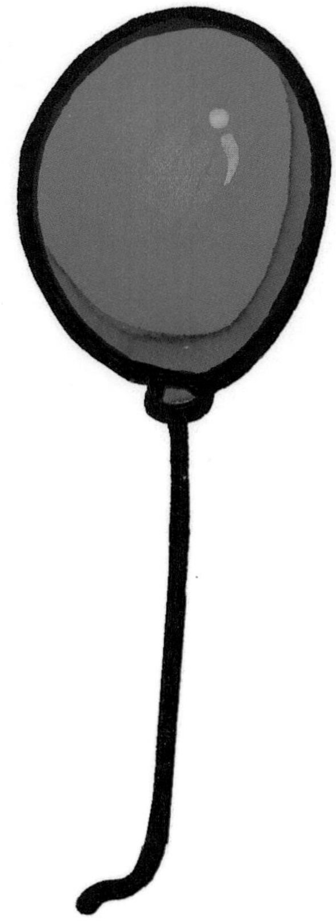

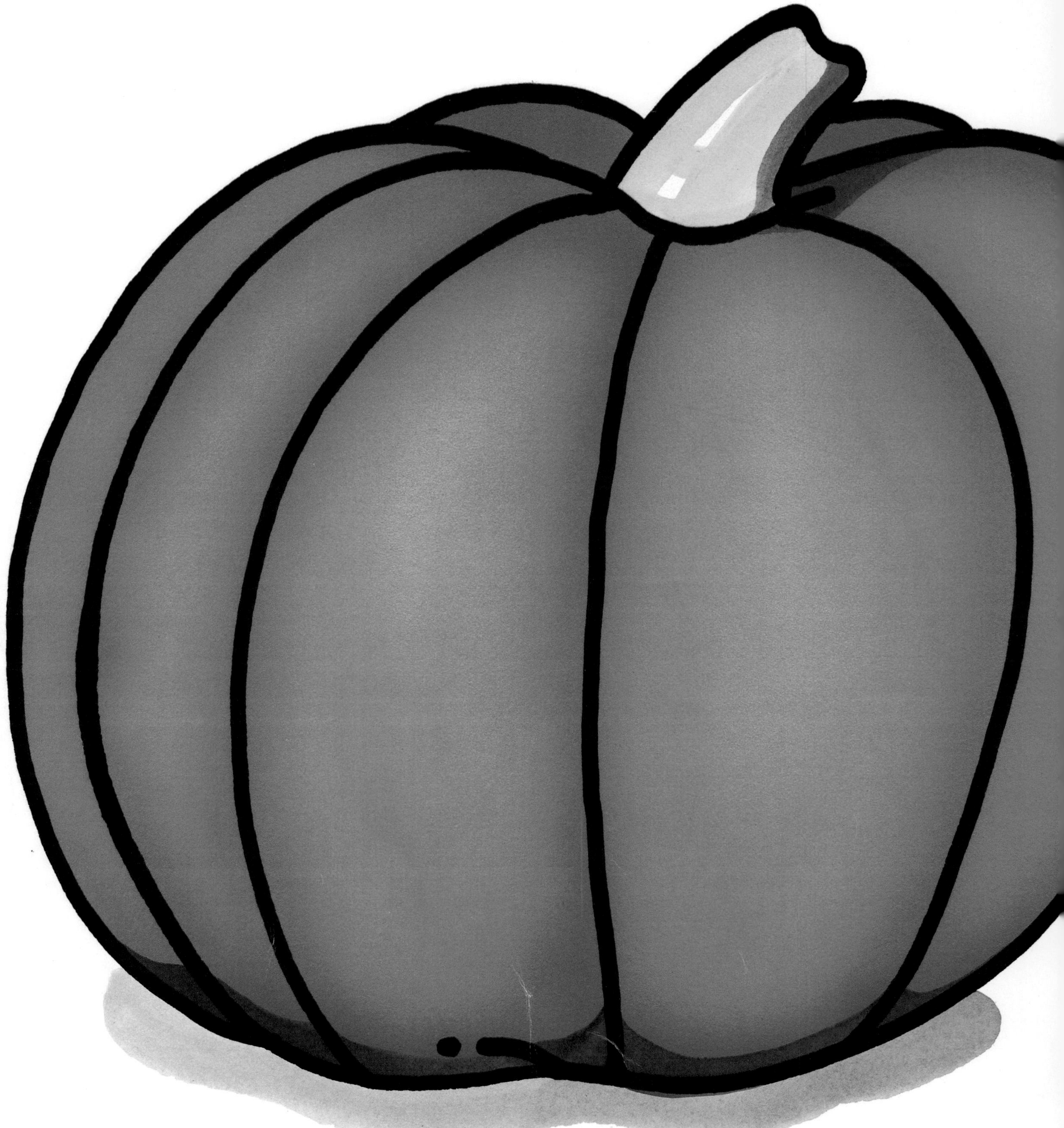

Large

Small

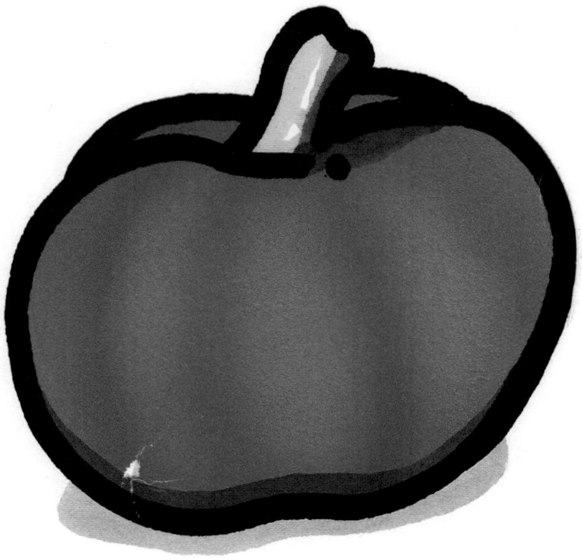

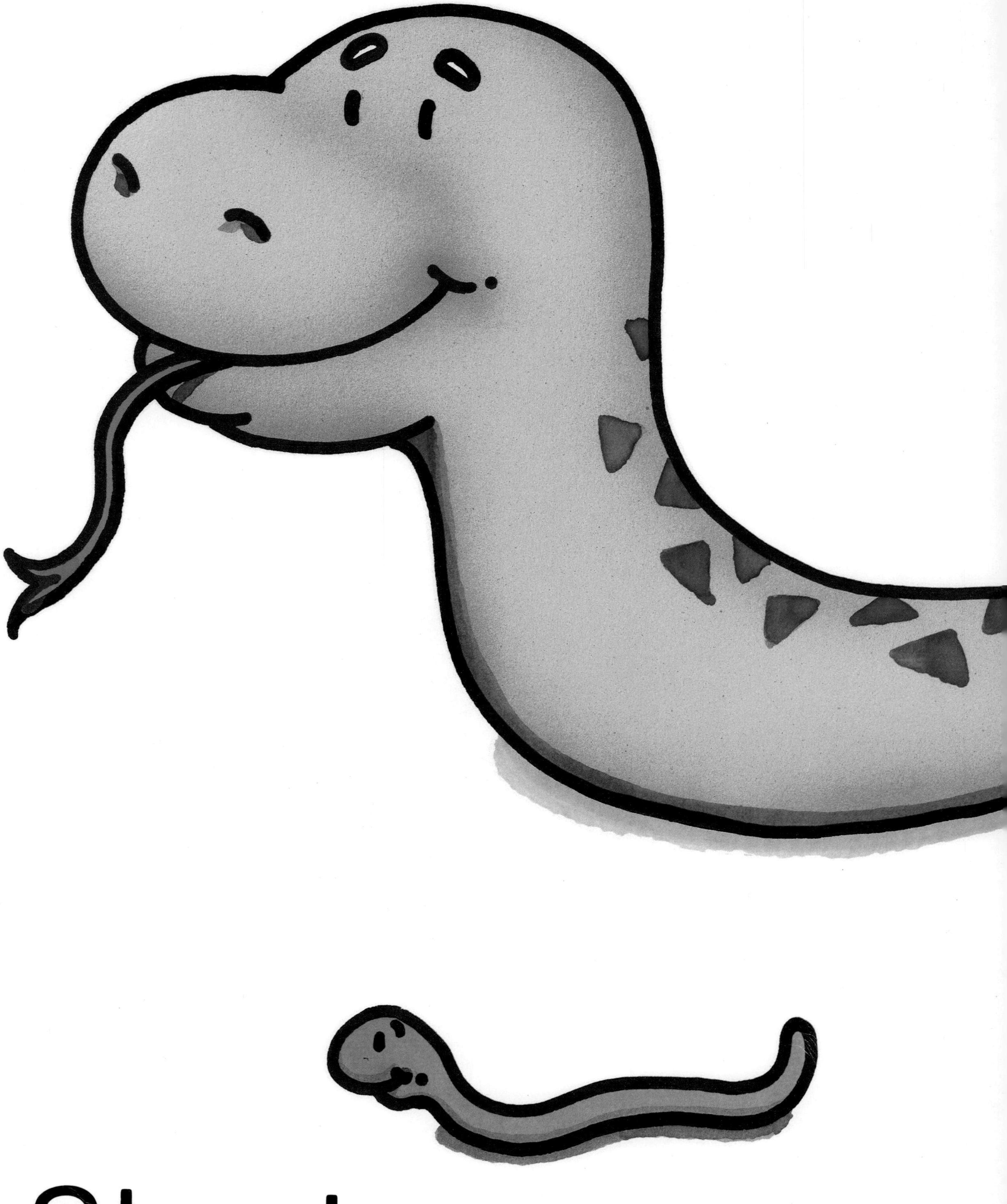

Short

Long

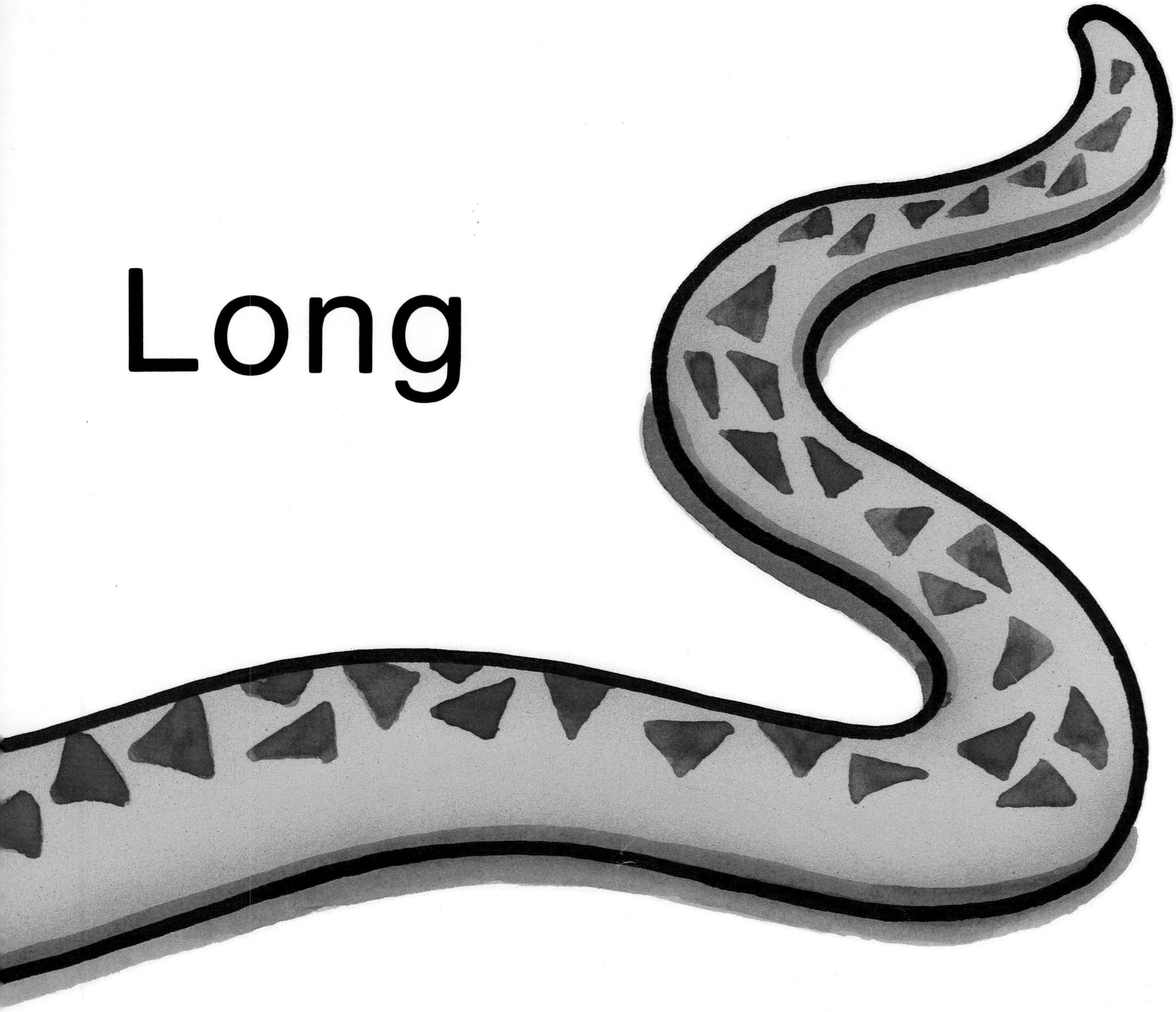

Long

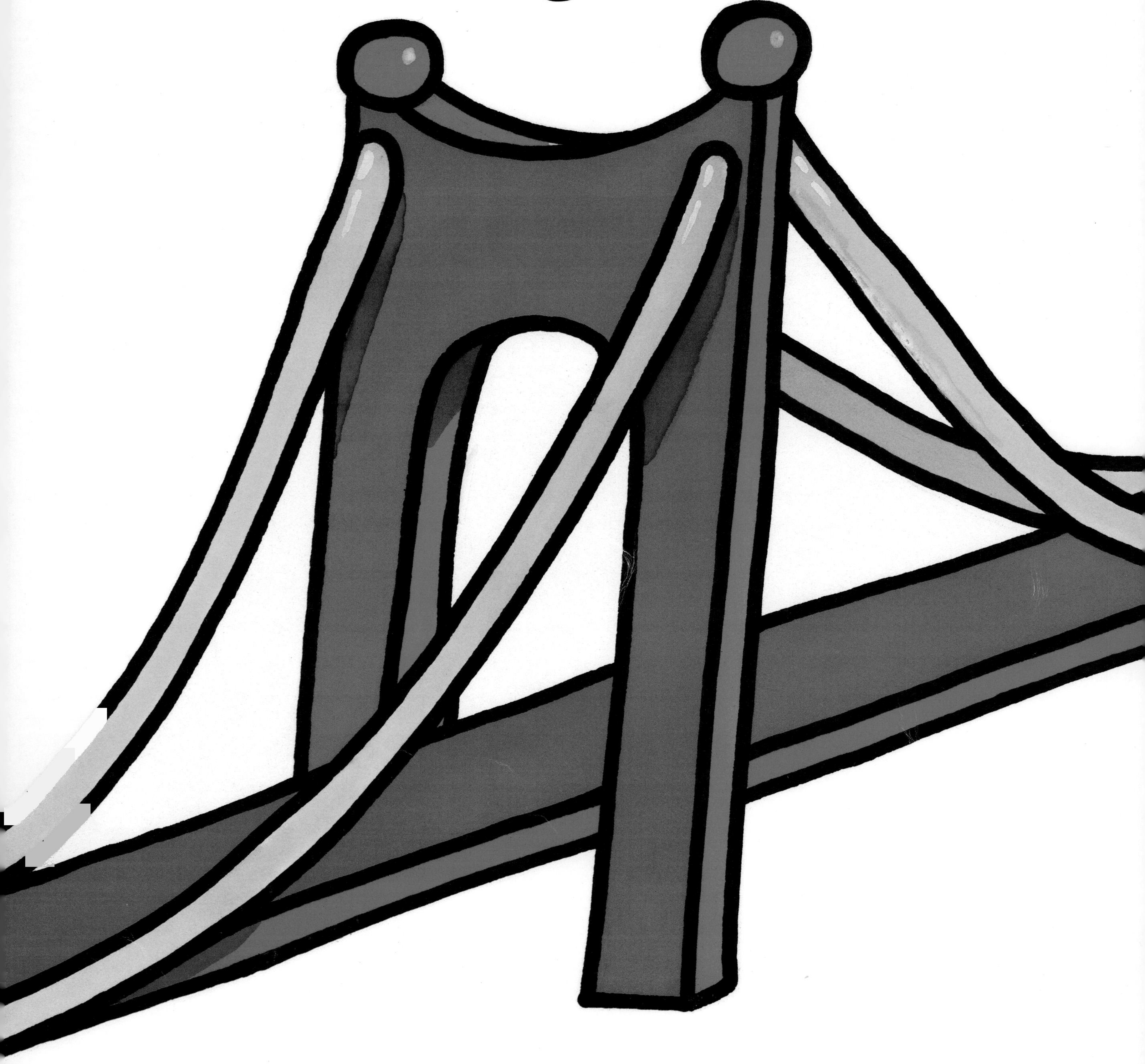

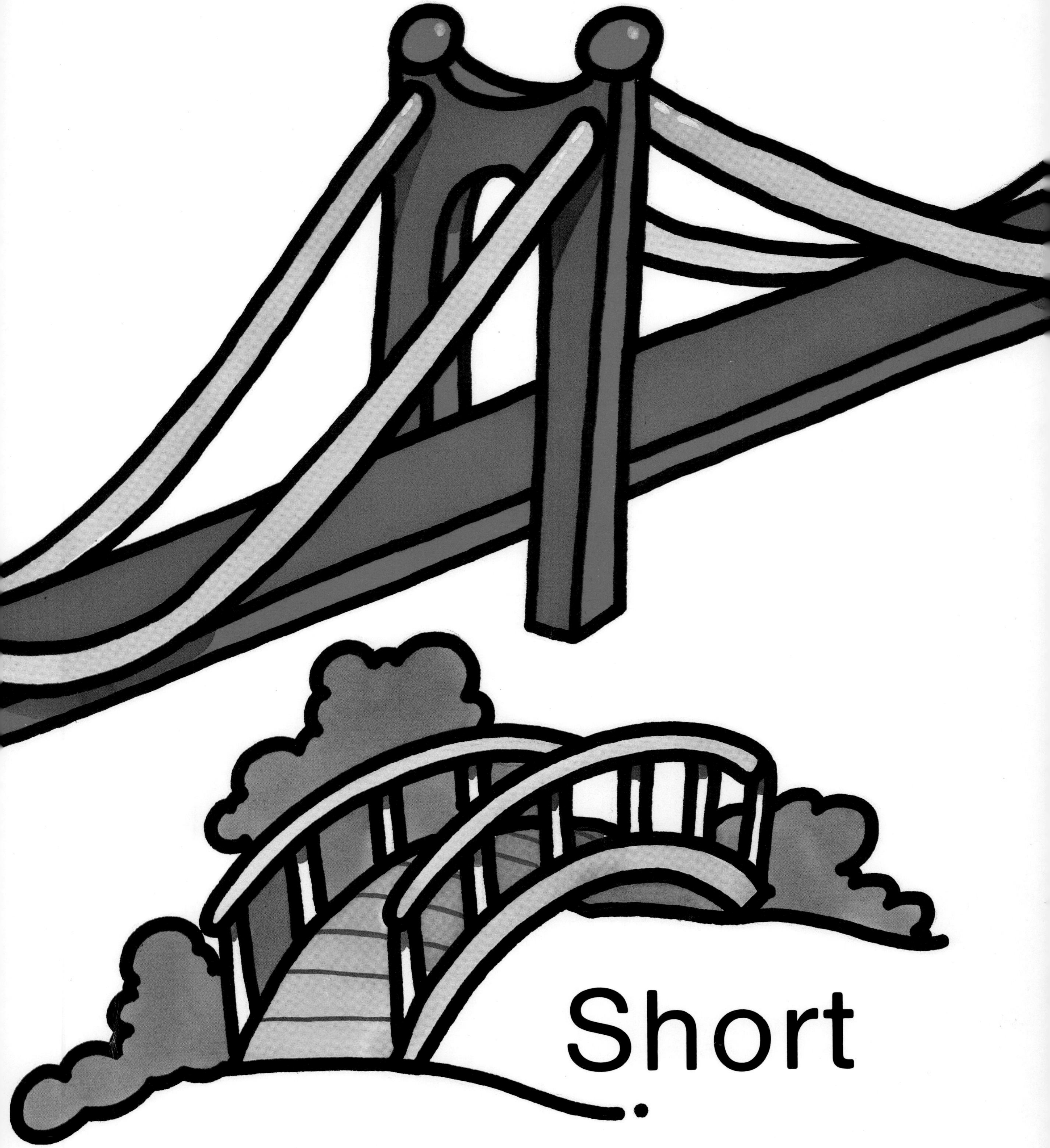

Short

Tall

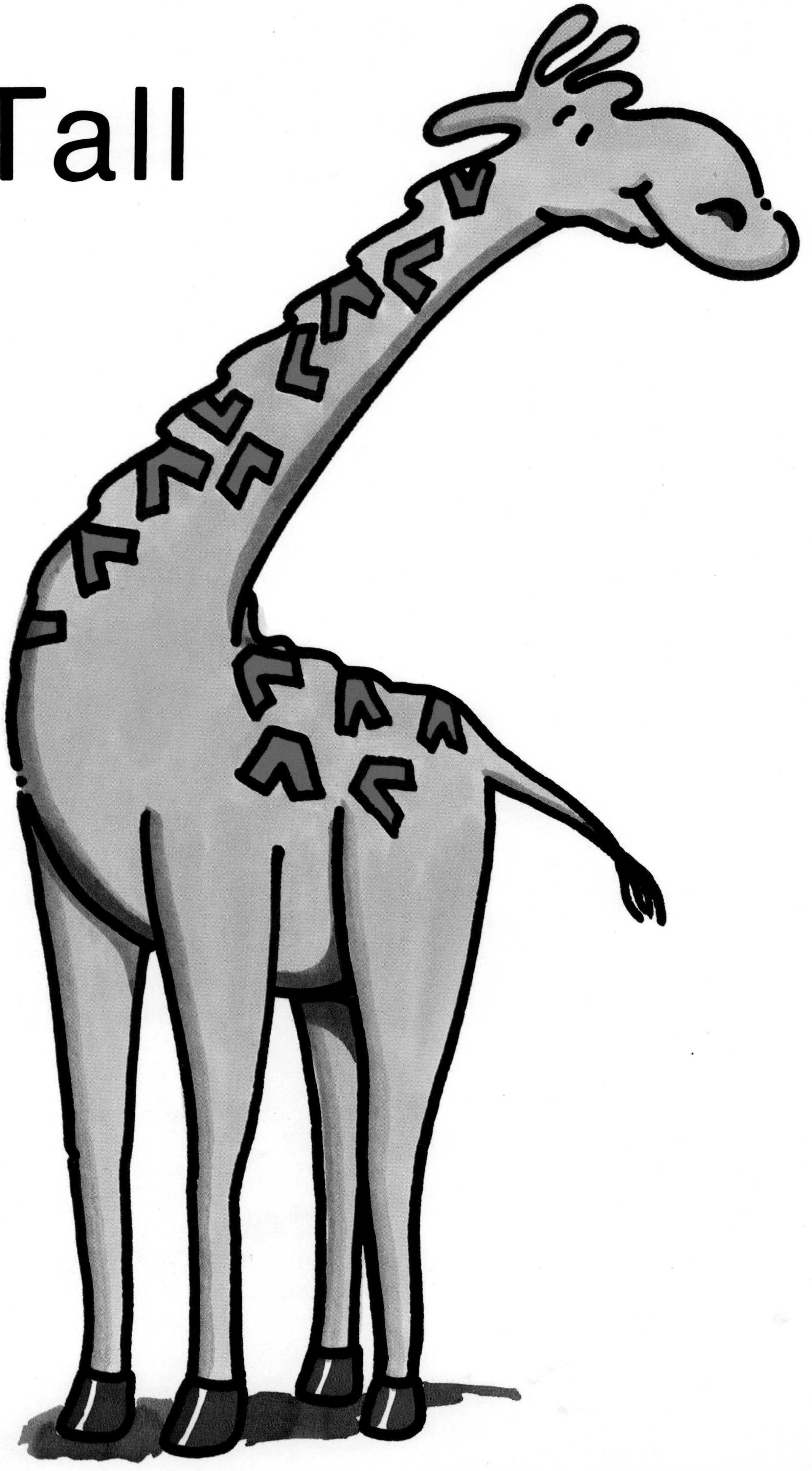

Short

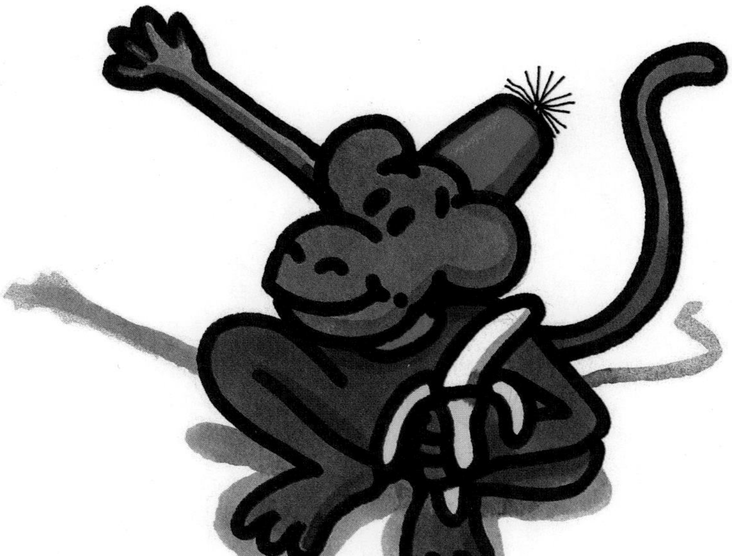

Large

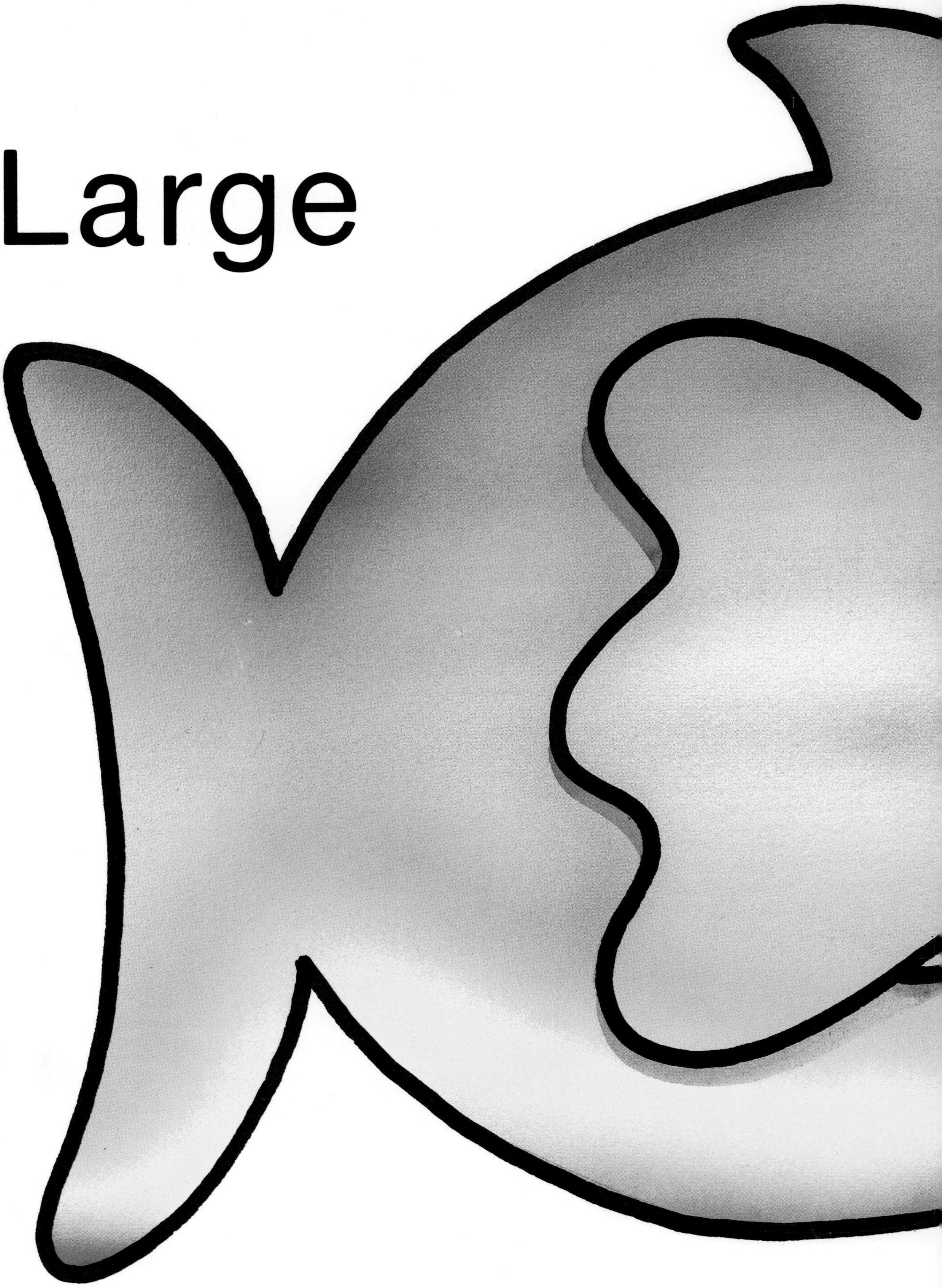

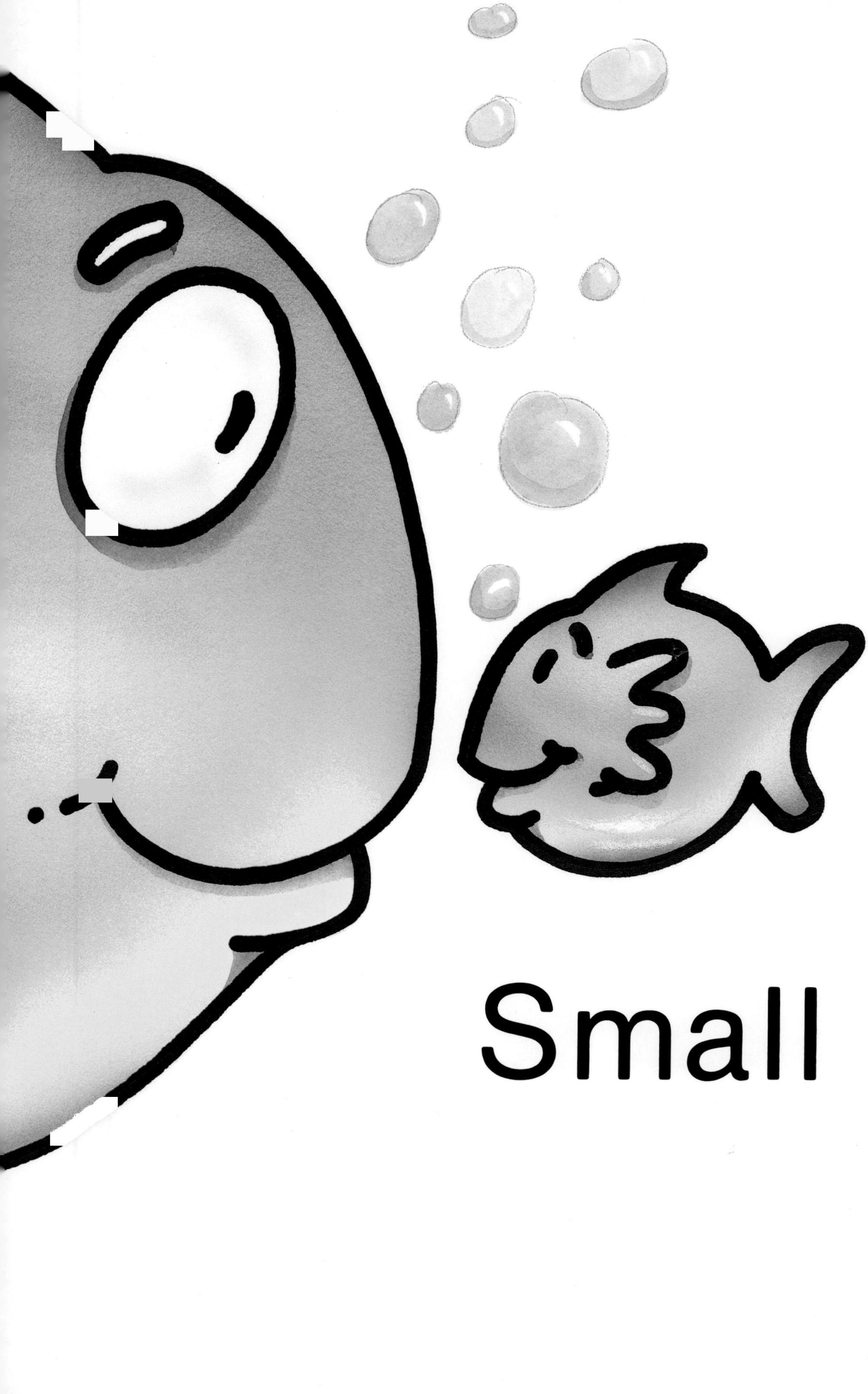

Small

Little

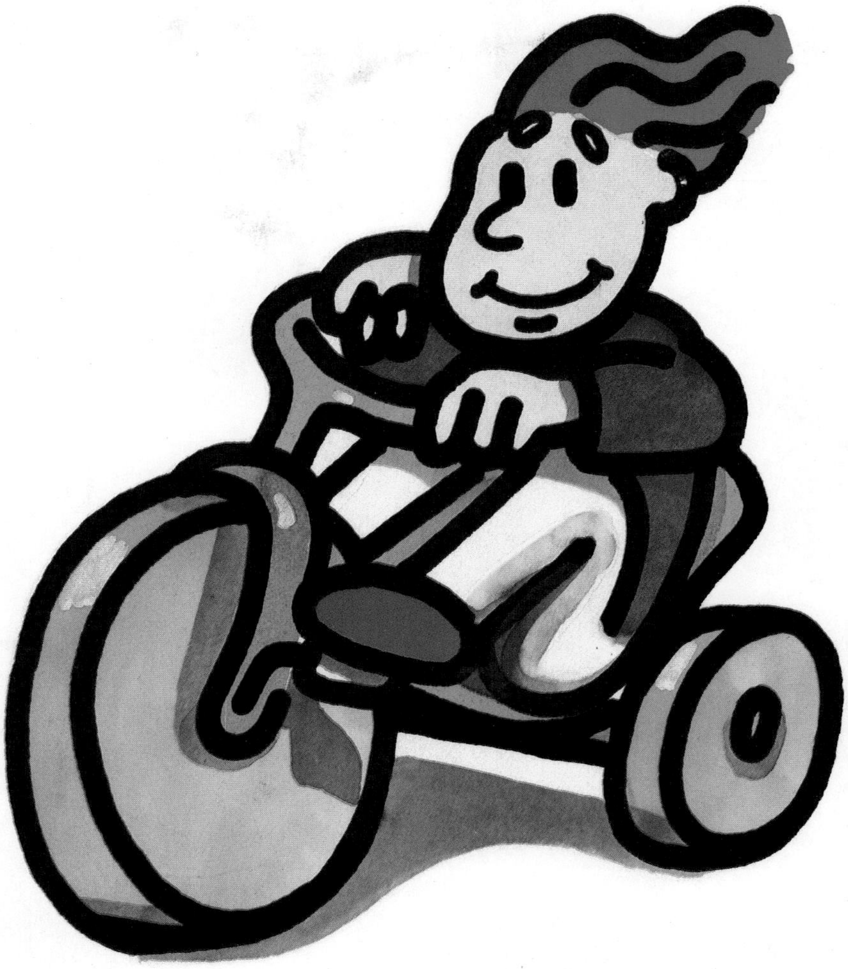

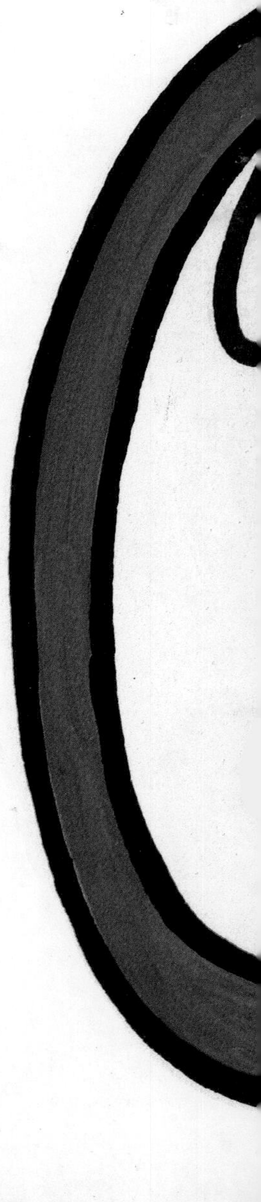